FLOWERS
for your
WEDDING DAY

FLOWERS
for your
WEDDING DAY

A Guide to Creating Beautiful
Bouquets, Arrangements & Decorations

DIANA TONKS

CB
CONTEMPORARY BOOKS
A TRIBUNE COMPANY

Library of Congress Cataloging-in-Publication Data

Tonks, Diana.
     Flowers for your wedding day : a guide to creating beautiful
bouquets, arrangements & decorations / Diana Tonks.
        p.   cm.
     Originally published: London : B. T. Batsford, 1994.
     Includes index.
     ISBN 0-8092-3061-5
     1. Wedding decorations.   2. Flower arrangements.   3. Bridal
bouquets.   I. Title.
SB449.5.W4T66   1997
745.92'6—dc20   96-30976
                                                   CIP

Cover design by Kim Bartko
Cover photograph copyright © Stewart Downie
Photographs on pages 38–39, 83–89 copyright © Diana Tonks
All other interior photographs copyright © Stewart Downie

This edition is reprinted by arrangement with B. T. Batsford Ltd.

Published by Contemporary Books
An imprint of NTC/Contemporary Publishing Company
Two Prudential Plaza, Chicago, Illinois 60601-6790
International Standard Book Number: 0-8092-3061-5
10   9   8   7   6   5   4   3   2   1

CONTENTS

Introduction 7

PLANNING THE FLOWERS

Visiting the florist 11
Choosing the flowers 12
Flowers for the bouquet 13
Looking after the flowers and foliage 13
Flowers for the ceremony 14
Flowers for the reception 15
Countdown to your wedding day 16

FLOWERS FOR THE BRIDE

Edwardian elegance 20
Christmas foliage 22
The bride's bedroom 24
A tied bouquet of lilies 26
A golden haze 28
Harvest flame 31
A delicate perfumed crown 34
A Bible or prayer book spray 36
Freesias and rosebuds 38

FLOWER GIRLS AND RINGBEARERS

Sumptuous baskets 42
Fun on the farm 46
In a field of flax 48
Little Bo-Peep 50

Flowers and pearls   52
Pomander balls and horseshoes   56
A floral hoop and crown   59

THE BRIDE & GROOM, AND GUESTS

A Christmas celebration   64
Flowers for the guests   67
Orchids for the bride and groom   71

OFF TO THE CHURCH

Lilies in a carriage   74
Vintage golden beauty   80
Flowers for a simple church   83
Flowers for a country church   90

FLOWERS FOR CELEBRATIONS

Wedding gifts and favors   96
Orchids on a cake   101
A floral luncheon at home   102
Strawberry tea   104

STEP-BY-STEP TECHNIQUES

A boutonniere   110
A rose corsage   112
A bride's or flower girl's headpiece   114
A handshower bouquet   116
A flower girl's nosegay   118
A front-facing arrangement   121

Acknowledgments   124
Index   126

ℐNTRODUCTION

Once upon a time, a bride would wear a traditional dress of cream or white; today you can choose any color or style you wish, and nothing would look out of place. We see marriage services taking place in churches, cathedrals and courthouses – and on paradise islands, amongst coral reefs, on top of mountains, or almost anywhere! Whatever the style of your wedding, wherever the ceremony is performed, this is your special day, your one chance to be princess for a day, and what better to complete the fairytale than perfect wedding flowers?

As well as their timeless beauty, flowers bring with them a rich tradition of symbolism. Flower circlets carried in the hand or floral crowns worn on the head echo the unbroken circle of the rings exchanged in the marriage service and symbolize eternal love and friendship; flower hoops for tiny bridesmaids are a pretty alternative to a hand-held nosegay. Traditionally red roses signify love; white lilies, purity; gardenia, femininity; and lily of the valley, happiness. Carnations speak of first love; the simple white daisy, in its pure, delicate form, represents innocence. Flowers speak a language all their own, and their hidden meaning can add a whole extra dimension to your choice of floral decoration. That is the romance – but creating it is another matter! This book will give you many ideas for beautiful arrangements for brides, bridesmaids, ringbearers, grooms, parents, guests, the travel arrangements, the ceremony, receptions, and presents. But it will also help you with all the practicalities, so you really can make your dreams come true. ❧

PLANNING
THE FLOWERS

*I*f you have decided to make your own floral arrangements, it is crucial that you plan things carefully. First acquire a small notebook and write everything down. List all the topics you need to cover. Jot down all your ideas, as you will not remember it all!

Without a doubt, you will need help. Make inquiries through family and friends. Ask them to recommend good florists, and willing helpers. You may need to recruit two or three helpers, depending on the workload and the speed with which they work.

Contact friends with gardens who could provide you with foliage. You can never have enough foliage, so it is worth acquiring more than you need: some varieties may take up water better than others, and at the last minute you will not have the time to look for alternative greenery.

Make all these plans several months beforehand, so everyone can keep their calendars free for you. Also set about buying or borrowing the materials you will need for your arrangements, to avoid any last minute panics. Here is a useful checklist.

- Dishes or plastic flower saucers for table centers. Larger bowls for other arrangements: you may be able to borrow these. There is usually a good stock of vases available in churches.
- Floral foam. Measure your dishes so you can cut the bricks of foam to size. You will find that the bricks are quite economical if you divide one up for use in two or three arrangements.
- A few floral foam "frogs" with sticky clay on the bottom for anchoring floral foam to the base of vases. Available from florists' and garden centers.
- Florists' wire. A useful thickness is 0.71 mm and should be 10 or 12 in (260 or 310 mm) long.

- Finer silver wires, or a spool of 0.28 mm or 0.32 mm wire, are crucial. All wires can be bought in small packs from florists' shops.
- Roll of floral foam sticky tape to tape the floral foam into the vase. It comes in green or white.
- Scissors.
- Small watering can and water sprayer.
- Buckets for conditioning your flowers and foliage.
- Flower preservative.
- Tape to cover wires.
- Chicken wire to cover floral foam, giving extra support for larger arrangements.
- If you are making your own bouquet, a floral foam bouquet holder (the dry foam version holds flowers best).
- Hot glue gun.
- Glue sticks.
- Bowl for cold water (for safety when using a glue gun).
- Drop cloth.
- Broom and dustpan; dust cloths.
- Ribbons for bows. Make up bows a few weeks before the wedding and store them in a plastic bag, somewhere dry and clean.

VISITING THE FLORIST

Whether you are planning to arrange all your wedding flowers, including the bouquets, or just some of them, your florist will be invaluable when buying the flowers and for general advice.

Visit your florist at least a couple of months before your wedding to find out which flowers will be available on your wedding date. If your florist is making arrangements for you it is advisable to book as early as possible: some florists take only one wedding booking a day.

Unless you are experienced in market buying, leave the wholesale markets alone. They are fun to visit and it is good to enjoy the hurly-burly. It would be a useful exercise to visit one to see what is available, but when it comes to buying, beware! You will have to buy in large quantities and there will be no one on hand to offer you time or advice as to what to buy and what not to buy. A florist, on the other hand, will sell you smaller quantities of flowers, and will have time to chat if you pick the right moment. Of course, a florist also opens at a more sociable time than the wholesale markets, which you would have to visit at around 5 A.M. in order to get the best choice!

CHOOSING THE FLOWERS

Obviously you will gather many ideas from magazines, and books like this one. Bridal fairs are more and more popular: there you will find everyone connected with weddings under one roof: jewelers, gentlemen's outfitters, cake decorators, photographers, dress designers, car rentals and florists.

Flowers are often one of the last things to be considered when planning a wedding. I suggest that you seek recommendations from friends and visit one or two florists before you settle on one: you will want to be looked after in a professional way, and feel comfortable with your choice. A good florist will have handled hundreds of weddings, and will enjoy discussing all your requirements, offering you expert help in choosing your flowers and color and style of arrangements.

By the time you see the florist you will probably have a good idea about what you do and do not like. It would be useful to take along a spare piece of your dress fabric, and the bridesmaid's too, or take a matching swatch of cotton. This will help the florist with the color choice, which is obviously crucial. Color is a difficult thing to carry in your mind and this is one occasion when you will want everything to be absolutely right.

Although you may desire a particular type of flower, also try to be guided by the experts as to which flowers will last longest: you will need everything to look fresh for the day. There is nothing worse than a wilting bouquet or headpiece. You will be quite warm and excited, and flowers worn on your body or head will soon wilt, so fresh, quality blooms are of paramount importance. The floral foam holders available for bouquet work will help; your flowers will not need to be handled so much, which will minimize bruising. Gluing techniques keep sap in the stem of the flower much longer; this also helps to keep flowers fresh.

When you have chosen your flowers, list your requirements and order your cut flowers at least a week before the wedding. Arrange to collect them on the Thursday if your wedding is on the Saturday. This will allow you plenty of time to give the flowers a good drink. There will also be time to look around elsewhere if you still require extra blooms. Remember, you will need all of Friday to arrange your flowers. Saturday needs to be left for you; there will be no time to worry about flower arranging on your wedding day itself. You could even pick your foliage as early as the Wednesday morning, giving it a long drink well before use. Keep all your flowers in a cool, dry place, away from direct light.

FLOWERS FOR THE BOUQUET

The bridal bouquet is the floral centerpiece of a wedding, and the style of dress will probably dictate the appropriate shape and color. You may have your heart set on a long hand-shower design incorporating natural trailing foliage, or you may want a simple tied bunch of country flowers. Whatever your choice, you should find that most flowers are available all year and can be flown in from around the world enabling you to choose the most exotic or the simplest of blooms. If you choose flowers that are out of season, you will usually have to pay a little extra for importing them.

Good choices for a bouquet include lily of the valley (*Convallaria majalis*) and stephanotis, sometimes called Madagascar jasmine or wax flower. Both are available throughout the seasons, as they can be greenhouse-grown, though they may be costly. Freesias, another favorite, can be found for most of the year, though not when the weather is too hot. Roses are with us all year round, in all colors, in miniature, and in sprays with several heads on. Honeysuckle (*Lonicera*) and clematis from the garden are perfect for a country look, but these seasonal flowers will only be available for a summer wedding.

LOOKING AFTER THE FLOWERS AND FOLIAGE

If you are picking flowers from the garden – do this a couple of days before the wedding – try to pick your foliage and flowers early in the morning just as the sap is starting to rise, before the sun shines on them. Cut all stems at an angle; thick stems should be split up with a pair of scissors. Do not hammer the stems, because this can encourage bacteria to form quickly, thus shortening the life of your flowers and foliage. Place your produce in large buckets of cold, clean water and add some flower preservative to keep the water fresh. Do not put too many stems into each bucket; allow them space to breathe. If you have any flowers in tight bud, place them in a bucket of warm (not hot) water, and this will encourage them to open a little more.

If you are buying cut flowers from the florist, put them in buckets of cold water in just the same way. Remember to recut the stems, which will have sealed up.

Foliage and flowers drink through their petals and leaves as well as through their stems. In their natural growing state they will absorb rainwater and moisture from the atmosphere. You will need to create this artificially by spraying the tops with a water mister. Do not drown the flowers – just a soft dusting of water droplets is all that

is required. If you allow too much water to settle in the center of flowers they will quickly deteriorate.

FLOWERS FOR THE CEREMONY

The marriage ceremony may not last very long, but the day would not be quite the same without flowers in the church or courthouse. This is the time when the bride and all the guests are seen in their full regalia as the whole wedding group stands together for the photographs. It may be possible to share the cost of the flowers with another bride if there are two weddings on the same day, allowing you to afford more flowers than perhaps you would have done. You will have to choose a selection of flowers that will blend with both your color schemes, or you can opt for pastel shades incorporating both your color choices. In a church it is nice to have formal arrangements on the altar, and perhaps a pedestal arrangement at the bottom of the chancel steps. If you want to go further then pew ends, arrangements on the font, on the window sills and around the pillars are striking. Whatever you choose rest assured that remaining flowers will always be enjoyed by those who attend Sunday worship, and may often be distributed among those who are ill in the parish.

Any of these church arrangements could be adapted for a courthouse wedding. Often there is a permanent display of artificial flowers already in the room. But if you want to provide a fresh display it can usually be accommodated: never hesitate to ask.

If your wedding is in a church, a few months before the wedding, get in touch with the officiant and find out the names of the people in charge of the flowers there. It may be that the church's flower committee will decorate the church for you, and you will simply choose the colors, or it may be that you are able to decorate the church yourself. Either way, they will be able to give you much advice.

The week before the wedding, check when it is convenient to get into the church: avoid working when there are services. Have all your containers with you, ready to use. The church flowers can be arranged early on the day before the wedding. The church will be cool, so everything should last well if you top off the water and spray your arrangements before you leave. For peace of mind ask one of your helpers to pop into the church on the wedding morning, just to check that everything is fine.

Be careful not to hammer or mark any woodwork, or move any furniture, without permission. Work on a large drop cloth so that all the mess can be cleared up easily.

Churches are often quite dark, with surroundings of wood and stone, so choose light, luminous flowers like white and cream, with a little added color, other than blue which tends to disappear into the background. Green foliage will help as a stabilizing influence when used as a background for the flowers.

FLOWERS FOR THE RECEPTION

Visit your reception venue well in advance of the wedding, and have a chat about the table layout, so you can decide how many arrangements you are going to need. If there are several round tables you may opt for nosegay shapes, but if the tables are long, you may choose a long and low design. A good deal will depend on your budget, so plan very carefully. In a hotel you may find that there are always flowers in the main reception areas, which will save you worrying about large pedestal displays. Quite often an allowance for flowers is included in your reception price, so do make inquiries to see if flowers are normally provided, and then discuss what you want with the manager. If you are using outside caterers for a reception at home, then the same decisions need to be made.

It is usually much better to have one or two large arrangements in a reception room, rather than half a dozen insignificant ones which will disappear in a room full of people. Be bold but tasteful; where you are working on a tight budget an arrangement can be enhanced with many different types of foliage: this will allow you to get away with fewer flowers. Remember foliage comes in many shapes and colors – variegated, golds, yellows, reds and varying shades of green. In a tall arrangement, you can gain extra height economically by using plumes of pampas grass (*Cortaderia*). They grow vigorously in the garden, and everyone knows someone with a pampas plant! When picked, treat it in the same way as any cut flower, placing the plumes in a deep bucket full of water. They do last quite some time, but after a few weeks will lose their fluffiness and may go to seed, shedding seeds everywhere – so be warned!

Table centers need only be small, neat, and compact as there is never enough space for all the glasses, napkins and cutlery on the table. A candle in the center of each display will elevate the arrangement. When using candles keep the flowers away as any foliage or flowers will obviously burn quickly and may cause a fire. If you do not wish to use candles then you may decide to add a little height with slightly taller flowers, but remember not to make your design too tall as the guests will want to talk over the flowers.

COUNTDOWN TO YOUR WEDDING DAY

As soon as you have decided to get married...	Book your church or courthouse, your reception venue and your florist. Book your limousine (do you want it decorated with flowers?); choose your cake design (do you want fresh or artificial flowers?); obtain samples of your dress material
Three to six months beforehand...	Visit your florist and start putting ideas together Arrange to meet the church flower committee List all the arrangements and work out how many flowers you need Contact everyone you need to help you Book a hairdresser for you and your bridesmaids, and discuss your requirements if you are having flowers in your hair
Two months beforehand...	Order the cut flowers from your florist. Gather together containers, floral foam, bouquet holders, wires, tape and all other materials; spare buckets, lots of plastic wrap and a decent pair of scissors Visit the reception venue and organize the flowers there Make up all the bows you need and store them in a plastic bag Make up artificial flower headpieces and cake-top
Two weeks beforehand...	Visit your florist and go through all the details of the final order; ensure the florist has all the correct dates and times of delivery Contact your helpers to make sure they are still available Confirm times with the hairdresser and the limousine: if you are decorating the limousine, make sure it will arrive early enough Visit your reception venue and discuss final plans
Four days beforehand...	Pick and condition your foliage and garden flowers
Three days beforehand	Prepare the dishes and containers. Tape in the floral foam and keep it moist

Two days beforehand...	Collect your cut flowers and empty flower boxes from the florist: the boxes are for storing your finished bouquet and boutonnieres
	Condition the cut flowers and put them in buckets full of clean cold water with flower preservative
	If the weather is not too hot, start the reception/home arrangements. Keep them in a cool, dry place, away from direct light
	Fill buckets with water and put in each one the correct quantity of flowers for one arrangement. Label each selection clearly, so that you know exactly what goes where on the day
The day before... Start early in the morning!	Meet your helpers at the church and tell them how you want it decorated. Start other helpers off on any outstanding arrangements and flowers for the limousine
	Make the arrangements for the wedding party. Put finished work in the prepared flower boxes, in this order: your bouquet; the bridesmaids' bouquets, hoops or baskets; the headpieces; the corsages; the boutonnieres
	Spray the flowers and cover everything in plastic wrap (see page 117). Store in a cool, dry place, away from strong sunlight
	Have pins ready for the corsages and boutonnieres. Do not put pins in overnight or they may rust
	Put all your home arrangements in position. Fill up with water and spray them gently
On the wedding day	Ask a helper to visit the church to check the flowers and top off with water. Ask another helper to deliver the reception and cake-top flowers, and another to attach the limo flowers
	The best man should collect the boutonnieres and corsages distribute them appropriately
	Lift the plastic wrap from the bouquets, etc., and check that flowers are fresh and crisp. Spray again if necessary, and re-cover lightly with plastic. Shake off any excess water before leaving for church
	Just before you leave for church, attach the headpieces
	Give the bridesmaids their bouquets and baskets, and finally pick up yours, and off you go!

FLOWERS
FOR THE BRIDE

ℰDWARDIAN ELEGANCE

THE FLOWERS

Fresh porcelain roses (*Rosa*)

Dried beech leaves (*Fagus*)

Dried lotus seed heads (*Nelumbo nucifera*)

An elegant, sophisticated Edwardian style dress in a peachy, cream silk trimmed with lace, is complemented by flowers of similar tone, carried in a long graceful hand shower. Porcelain-colored roses are the only fresh flowers used here, combined with gilded dried lotus seed heads (*Nelumbo nucifera*), backed by golden dusted beech (*Fagus*) leaves. I chose a banana-fiber ribbon in pale peach with a gold thread running through it, to complement the golden leaves and dried heads. Using dried and fresh material together creates a stunningly beautiful design.

This design is assembled on a foam bouquet holder (see pages 116–7) and the flowers and seed heads glued in place. For the gilded effect I used a gold spray paint and gently misted each piece required. (Always remember to spray out of doors, as the fumes released can be quite intense. Spray each piece separately on a piece of newspaper to ensure that you do not spray anything you did not mean to spray. And make sure the material you choose is completely dry so that the paint adheres.) The seed heads and beech leaves were wired on strong support wires, as were the ribbon bows and trails. I also wired one or two of the longer roses leaving them on their natural stems to give them extra support.

A side spray worn in the hair matches all the flowers used in the bouquet. To make one, wire each piece into small groups and glue to a comb, which will keep it in place on the head. ✑

CHRISTMAS FOLIAGE

Glorious shades of green foliage are blended together into a cascading wild bouquet. The choice of material for a design like this is endless: here there is perfume too from sprigs of sage (*Salvia officinalis*) and rosemary (*Rosmarinus officinalis*), which are thought to bring good luck.

Christmas walnuts (*Juglans*), painted gold, give the bouquet a focal point and lead your eye down the green and gold ribbon to trails of ivy (*Hedera*) and butcher's broom (*Ruscus*). The bride's head is crowned with a circle of foliage, golden walnuts and ribbon. ❧

THE FLOWERS

Rosemary (*Rosmarinus officinalis*)

Ivy (*Hedera*)

Hebe (figwort shrub)

Jerusalem sage (*Phlomis fruticosa*)

Sage (*Salvia officinalis*)

Butcher's broom (*Ruscus*)

Euonymus (*E. fortunei*)

Poinsettia (*Euphorbia*) foliage

Golden walnuts (*Juglans*)

THE *B*RIDE'S BEDROOM

On the morning of the wedding there is great excitement in the air – a cup of tea is called for to calm the nerves! A gorgeous arrangement of orange lilies (*Lilium*), with a backing of bay (*Laurus nobilis*), hebe and ivy (*Hedera*) foliage displayed so stunningly in this old copper samovar, originally used in Russia as a tea urn, bring the bedroom to life. Foliage forms the outline, but doesn't overtake the design, only on the left-hand side when the ivy spills over the edge. ❧

THE FLOWERS

Orange lilies (*Lilium*)

Ivy (*Hedera*)

Hebe (figwort shrub)

Bay tree or Laurel (*Laurus nobilis*)

A TIED BOUQUET OF LILIES

A simple hand-tied bouquet of peach and cream lilies (*Lilium*) – perfect blooms, opening to their fullest. The lilies look splashed with droplets of fresh morning dew. The unopened buds are important too, adding another dimension, texture and shape to the design.

To make a tied bouquet, leave each flower on its natural stem and place and hold each piece in one hand. Start with a stem of foliage at the center, adding flowers and foliage one at a time, working outward. You will have to cross your stems to keep them in place. Use string to bind the stems where you have been holding them and finish around the outer edge with foliage. To cover the string as here, tie a large fluffy green banana-fiber ribbon bow with extra trails. Trim the unwanted stalks from the bottom of your bouquet, and if the design is well balanced it *should* then stand up on its stalks on the table! To keep this bouquet fresh stand upright in a bucket partly filled with water. Do not lay it on its side for too long, as it will lose its circular shape. ﻬ

THE FLOWERS

Peach and cream lilies (*Lilium*)

Ivy (*Hedera*)

Hebe (figwort shrub)

A GOLDEN HAZE

Yellow heralds spring, and golden double tulip blooms (*Tulipa*) glow brightly here amidst white tulips, scented white lilac (*Syringa vulgaris*) and broom (*Genista*), relieved by delicate soft green snowball bush (*Viburnum opulus* "Roseum") foliage. Perfume wafts gently from the flowers, enhancing their beauty: it always makes such a difference if the flowers are scented.

This bouquet was assembled using wires (like the nosegay on pages 118–9). Where possible I left the flowers on their natural stems and just support-wired them discretely on the outside. Ribbon is not an essential part of this bouquet but I felt that the watermarked taffeta added a perfect finishing touch. If you are using ribbon, it is best to add it at the very last minute, otherwise, like me, you will find yourself ironing the ribbon just before the bride goes off to church.

Wire all your main flowers on black florist wires using support wire where necessary. Tape everything using the same color tape throughout; i.e., all green or white or natural. When you have wired and taped everything, stand the finished flowers and leaves upright in a weighted container to lessen bruising, taking one at a time from the container and placing it into the bouquet, taping firmly as you go. There is a very little foliage used here – only that of the snowball bush and tulip leaves – making this a truly floral bouquet.

To make the bouquet, start at the tail end with a bud or tighter flower, adding different flowers one at a time, interspersing them as they will appear throughout the design. Work your way up until you come to the point which will be the center of the bouquet. Now bend the wires down to form the start of the handle. Add the side pieces, taking the flowers back over your hand to cover the handle.

Now wire and tape together the units of flowers and foliage (see pages 118–9), and bring them into the design. The central and focal blooms should be introduced last.

THE FLOWERS

Double yellow tulips (*Tulipa*)

White tulips (*Tulipa*)

Snowball bush (*Viburnum opulus* "Roseum")

Broom (*Genista*)

Euonymus (*E. fortunei*)

Ivy (*Hedera*)

White lilac (*Syringa vulgaris*)

The ribbon can be placed in position as late as possible. Cover the bouquet handle with ribbon, by taping a long wire down the handle so that it points out at the end, and winding your ribbon around the handle from about halfway down, working downward. When you reach the additional long wire take your ribbon down on to it and then bend the wire neatly back up against the handle, which will secure the end and stop the ribbon slipping off at the bottom and unravelling. Continue taking your ribbon round and round, working upward now, covering all the wires and all the handle. Pin, glue or sew it at the top as high up under the flowers as is possible. Finally make a neat ribbon bow and glue or pin it into place to finish it all off neatly.

The bridesmaid's bouquet is made in just the same way but with less material so that it is smaller than the bride's. Crown headpieces (see pages 114–5) can be worn low on the head like the brim of an Easter bonnet. ❧

THE FLOWERS

Double yellow tulips (*Tulipa*)

White tulips (*Tulipa*)

Snowball bush (*Viburnum opulus* "Roseum")

Broom (*Genista*)

Euonymus (*E. fortunei*)

Ivy (*Hedera*)

White lilac (*Syringa vulgaris*)

$\mathcal{H}$ARVEST FLAME

The deepest, richest red and orange lilies (*Lilium*) and matching roses are interspersed with gilded fresh green corn and artificial fruit. The fruit adds lots of interest and looks good enough to eat! The lilies and roses set the bouquet alight, a perfect foil to a creamy dress. A headpiece of matching gilded corn in a circlet or crown is the perfect finishing touch.

This hand shower is again designed in a floral foam holder. There is a slight difference in the technique used here from that which was used to create the nosegay design (page 119), namely, you must support wire the longer, more vulnerable stems of roses and lilies, which then need to be glued in place firmly. This technique creates a natural lightweight bouquet, and shortens the time you need to handle the flowers.

To make the crown, first measure around the bride's head with a tape measure, string or ribbon to find a comfortable size. Lay the corn in a circle on the table to assess how much you will need, then cut all the heads off the corn. Using only the stalks, bind them with wire into the correct sized circle, and when you have finished, spray it with gold spray paint. Then, with a hot glue gun, stick on each head of corn, using two or three side by side to create a deep crown, working around in a circle and making sure every piece lies in the same direction. When the first row is glued on, start another row on top, continuing until the crown looks thick and full enough. Finish off by spraying here and there with gold paint, leaving small areas of natural green showing through. Leave to dry. It may be necessary to add one or two extra heads the next day to cover up any wires still showing. Often things look quite different when you leave them and return the next day with a fresh pair of eyes, so it is worth not leaving this one to the last minute. This could of course be made weeks before the wedding! ❧

THE FLOWERS

Orange roses (*Rosa*)

Orange lilies (*Lilium*)

Corn

Artificial apples and raspberries

A DELICATE PERFUMED CROWN

Laid on an ivory veil edged in handmade cotton lace, this crown of lush greens and cream looks almost as if each flower is hand-painted porcelain. A blush of deep brown rouge touches the younger flowers. To create this I used a circle of taped wire, bound with natural trails of ivy. I wired on pieces of laurustinus (*Viburnum tinus*) and looped lily of the valley leaves (*Convallaria majalis*) next; then glued on grouped stems of lily of the valley and finally the heads of Lenten roses (*Helleborus orientalis*) in their colors of late spring. ❧

THE FLOWERS

Lenten roses (*Helleborus orientalis*)

Laurustinus (*Viburnum tinus*)

Ivy (*Hedera*)

Lily of the valley (*Convallaria majalis*)

34

A BIBLE OR PRAYER BOOK SPRAY

A simple but small spray carried on a Bible or prayer book offers an unusual alternative for brides who choose not to carry a large bouquet. This prayer book whose inscription dates from 1917, uses a bookmark of antique lace to which the flowers have been attached.

The spray is made with a length of satin ribbon or lace. You need to leave the tail of ribbon inside the book longer than the one on top: open the book at the marriage service and place the long end of ribbon like a bookmark, and bring the other end over the top of the book. If using satin ribbon keep the shiny side up by twisting the piece inside the book to show the right side. Stitch the two tails of ribbon where they meet the edge of the book, keeping the ribbon as tight as possible over the front of the book. Pull the sewn piece up into the body of the book to conceal the join.

This spray is made with ivy leaves (*Hedera*) and lily of the valley (*Convallaria majalis*). One or two stems are wired just to add a little extra support at the length. To wire the lily of the valley, insert a thin silver wire up into the end of the stem, and work upward, twisting around gently. When you come to the last bud at the top, take the wire around a couple of times, and cut off the remaining wire as close to the flower bud as possible so it will not catch on the wedding dress. When you first try this you may find that just as you get to your last bud and start to twist your wire, off it falls, so you will then have to go down to the next bud and try again. You may have to practice a few times to get it right.

Ivy forms the backing of this spray: add to it each piece of lily of the valley, building it up in your hand; then tie the bunch with a ribbon bow and sew it to the lace. Leave this until the very last minute so as not to damage the prayer book with water.

From each stem of tiny white waxy bells a fragrant scent drifts through the air surrounding the spray. What a joy! ❧

THE FLOWERS

Lily of the valley (*Convallaria majalis*)
Ivy (*Hedera*)

$\mathcal{F}$REESIAS AND ROSEBUDS

THE FLOWERS

Lemon freesias

White roses (*Rosa*)

Miniature lemon rose buds (*Rosa*)

White spray carnations (*Dianthus caryophyllus*)

Gypsophila (*G. paniculata*)

Orchids (*Dendrobium*)

Bear grass (*Dasylirion*)

Sword fern (*Nephrolepis exaltata*)

Fern (*Arachniodes*)

Ivy (*Hedera*)

Tiny lemon rosebuds and larger single white roses, mingle with white spray carnations (*Dianthus*), strongly scented lemon freesias and with white orchids (*Dendrobium*) in a very pretty design. Dainty heads of gypsophila (*G. paniculata*) peep out between the other flowers like tiny delicate beads. The foliage consists of ivy (*Hedera*) trails, sword fern (*Nephrolepis exaltata*) and bear grass (*Dasylirion*) used in loops and strands. Spray carnations are smaller than single-headed carnations but are not so bulky and easier to use in bouquet work.

The bridesmaid's bouquet is a crescent design which is made like a very large handbag spray, as if you were joining two very large corsages together. Instead of making a straight "corsage," start at one tip, slightly curving as you move upward, and when you get to the end (the middle of the crescent), bend your handle back and down. Put that curve of flowers to one side (to minimize bruising I stand mine in a wine bottle, filled with sand to weight it). Follow the same procedure with the other curve, this time bending your flowers the other way. To join the two together you need wire – bind where the two handles meet and complete by adding the focal flower. On the morning of the wedding cover the handles with ribbon and finish with a matching bow at the back. ✒

FLOWER GIRLS AND RINGBEARERS

SUMPTUOUS BASKETS

Coral Transvaal daisies (*Gerbera*) and roses, broken by tiny heads of white heath (*Aster ericoïdes*) create a simple but striking design set in a country basket of tumbling ivy leaves. A bride and flower girl can carry two matching flat baskets, one a little smaller for the flower girl. Glue a round plastic dish into the basket, using a slightly larger dish for the bride to support her mass of flowers. Cut a piece of floral foam to fit the dish and soak it quite quickly so as not to make it too heavy. Tape it securely to the dish to ensure there are no disasters: remember that not everyone will handle flowers with the care that you do, and your heart may jump into your mouth if you see a small flower girl swinging your beautiful work of art around and around!

To make up the basket arrangement, first cover the foam with small pieces of foliage, overhanging the dish to hide it. Then position long pieces of ivy at one end so that they flow out over the rim of the basket; then add the Transvaal daisies, followed by the roses. Break up the strong color by interspersing the delicate white heath. To balance the arrangement, take any discarded stalks and put them in the other end of the basket, to give the impression of a freshly picked bunch of flowers. Tidy up the stems by trimming them evenly. Finish by placing a bow of matching coral fabric, which I would first wire and then tape, into the foam where the flowers and foliage meet. Make sure that you cannot see any foam or the dish at the stalks end; if you can, then you will need to add small clumps of foliage until it is all covered.

The matching headpieces for the bride and flower girl are wired into a small spray and glued to a comb. I glued extra single daisy heads to the end to cover all the mechanics. ✺

THE FLOWERS

Coral roses (*Rosa*)

Transvaal daisies (*Gerbera*)

Heath (*Aster ericoïdes*)
Wild ivy (*Hedera*) with its flowers and fruit

42

THE BASKET

Coral roses (*Rosa*)

Transvaal daisies (*Gerbera*)

Heath (*Aster ericoïdes*)

Wild ivy (*Hedera*) with its flowers
and fruit

THE HEADPIECE

Coral roses (*Rosa*)

Heath (*Aster ericoïdes*)

Wild ivy (*Hedera*)

$\mathcal{F}$UN
ON THE FARM

**THE BRIDE'S AND RINGBEARERS'
FLOWERS**

Silk polyester flowers

Fresh laurustinus (*Viburnum
tinus*) foliage

**THE FLOWERS ON THE GATE AND
WALL**

Butcher's broom (*Ruscus*)

White carnations (*Dianthus*)

Heath (*Aster ericoïdes*)

Ivy (*Hedera*)

A whimsical scene on a cold morning in January, brightened by the ringbearers' colorful satin suits, this gorgeous golden color echoed in the arm bouquet carried by the bride. All these flowers were artificial, for the bride to keep them just as they were on her wedding day. (These can also be a boon if you suffer from hay fever.)

This is a tied arm bouquet, using fresh foliage of laurustinus (*Viburnum tinus*). Hold the flowers in your hand and introduce each bloom and piece of foliage one at a time, feeding the stems through each other and crossing them as you go. When you come to the center use a little more foliage to raise up the focal flowers, tie firmly without damaging the flowers and complete the bouquet with a large full bow, remembering to trim the stems evenly.

The headpiece is made from artificial cream roses, using a wire crown made to fit the bride's head (see page 59), with the roses wired to the frame at the front, and the back bound in ribbon to cover the wires. The boys' boutonnieres are matching artificial roses.

The old wooden gate is decorated with a dainty garland of butcher's broom (*Ruscus*), ivy (*Hedera*) and tiny heads of heath (*Aster ericoïdes*). The butcher's broom is simply intertwined with the ivy, the pieces of foliage twisted together until the length is right. Small daisies are wired in between, with bows of thin white ribbon trailing down, breaking up the dullness of the wooden slats and the dark foliage.

The arrangement on the wall is displayed in a heavy terra-cotta bowl; its matching foliage and white carnations dotted again with the little daisy flowers. The bowl holds bricks of floral foam, taped across to hold them firmly in the breeze. This is an arrangement best done *in situ*, so that the ivy trails cascade down over the bricks. A glint of light reflects off the bright green moss, which has lived undisturbed on the wall for years. ❧

$\mathcal{I}$N A FIELD OF FLAX

TIED BUNCH

Delphiniums

Prairie gentians (*Eustoma grandiflorum*)

Gladioli

Foxgloves (*Digitalis*)

THE FLOWER GIRL'S BASKET

Peruvian lilies (*Alstroemeria*)

Pinks (*Dianthus*)

Cornflowers (*Centaurea*)

Lady's mantle (*Alchemilla*)

Gypsophila (*G. paniculata*)

THE RINGBEARER'S FLOWER

Lady's mantle (*Alchemilla*)

Cornflower (*Centaurea*)

This bride is carrying a tied bunch of mixed summer flowers. Delphiniums have been laid at the back, and there is no foliage used here at all. Gladioli, foxgloves (*Digitalis*) and prairie gentians (*Eustoma grandiflorum*) are gathered up, one flower stem at a time and placed next to the delphiniums, then tied together at the assembly point with ribbon or string to form a very natural tied arm bunch. The bouquet looks almost as if it has just been gathered from the garden and placed across the bride's arm. To finish off I tied a large bow, made from the same fabric used in the wedding dress, to cover the ribbon or string. The bride wears a half-band of flowers in her hair, with lady's mantle (*Alchemilla*) and gypsophila (*G. paniculata*) glued on the band first, followed by bold, single heads of delphinium flowers.

The flower girl is carrying a tiny basket arrangement designed in floral foam. Plastic wrap placed inside the basket acts as a waterproof lining. The flowers here are pinks (*Dianthus*), cornflowers (*Centaurea*), Peruvian lilies (*Alstroemeria*), gypsophila and lady's mantle. To assemble a basket like this treat it in just the same way as you would for any floral arrangement. The design should be balanced all around, but try not to make it too heavy. Choose dainty flowers and just moisten the floral foam rather than soaking it, which will help to keep it light in weight. To finish off, wire a number of trails of thin blue ribbon together to tumble out of the front of the basket. A little spray of matching flowers, glued to a small circle of thin card, is pinned to the hat – to do the same, first cover the card base by gluing lady's mantle into place, add a little gypsophila, and finish by gluing two or three single flower heads from the stem of a delphinium. The ringbearer carries a tiny bunch of cornflowers and lady's mantle tied together with matching blue ribbon.

ℒITTLE BO-PEEP

THE FLOWERS

Coral roses (*Rosa*)

Snowball bush (*Viburnum opulus* "Roseum")

Broom (*Genista*)

Gypsophila (*G. paniculata*)

A truly stunning idea for a country wedding – flowers in the hair and crook bedecked with flowers. The effect is dramatic, and the hair is especially nice, as in church all the guests see during the service is the back of everyone's head. The flowers in the hair were wired sprays of gypsophila (*G. paniculata*), broom (*Genista*), single rose heads and clusters of soft green snowballs (*Viburnum opulus* "Roseum"). Each piece was then taped and the wire cut down to a length of about two inches: the hairdresser did the rest! Each flower is woven into a French braid, and the braid finished off with a cream bow at the bottom. Always remember that the head loses a lot of heat which means that flowers will wilt quicker if woven into the hair, so try to ensure this is left until the last minute before the wedding, enabling the flowers to remain fresh for the maximum amount of time.

You can buy crooks in all sizes, but I made this one by using a garden cane which I cut to the right size for the flower girl. I inserted a wire coat hanger into the top of the cane and bent it around to make the curve at the top of the crook, then covered the whole thing in cream ribbon, gluing every now and then as I went. I wired the groups of flowers together in the same way as a corsage, and made two sprays, one for each side – if the flowers go all the way around then it does not matter which way a child holds it for the photographs! A large cream bow wired on with strips of ribbon and pearls tumbling down adds the final touch. ☙

FLOWERS AND PEARLS

On a blustery but happy, flower-filled day in May, a beautiful bridal posy design of roses, Peruvian lilies (*Alstromeria*) and freesias is an attractive alternative to a full bouquet.

It is designed on a floral foam bouquet holder; to create a similar posy, start at the outer edge by pushing each stem into the foam, and gluing each flower and piece of foliage in place in turn, until the

THE FLOWERS

Pink roses (*Rosa*)

Ivy (*Hedera*)

Jerusalem sage (*Phlomis fruticosa*)

Purple freesias

Peruvian lilies (*Alstroemeria*)

52

outer circle is complete. Then work from the focal point in the center, filling the round shape completely with flowers and greenery. It isn't necessary to glue every stem, mainly the prominent and outer flowers.

To add a delicate touch to this nosegay I wired tiny strings of pearls into bows, and placed them in the middle when the design was complete. I also glued rosebuds firmly to strings of pearls which hung from the front of the nosegay, giving extra movement and interest to the design. I used the deeper colored Peruvian lilies in recess, keeping the roses and freesias more prominent. The colors of the flowers blend with the floral fabric of the flower girl's dress, and I created a smaller version of the bride's nosegay for the flower girl to carry.

Their matching headpieces were made up using the same selection of flowers, with each flower and leaf wired and then taped into a small spray, with wired pearl bows added as before and with a string of pearls bound around the completed spray. To secure the headpieces in place, I glued them on to combs. ❧

THE FLOWERS

Pink roses (*Rosa*)

Ivy (*Hedera*)

Jerusalem sage (*Phlomis fruticosa*)

Purple freesias

Peruvian lilies (*Alstroemeria*)

POMANDER BALLS AND HORSESHOES

Pomander balls have long been a popular alternative flower girls' floral design, particularly for younger flower girls. Once they were made up of hundreds of single spray chrysanthemum heads (*Dendranthema*) or tiny petals of feathered carnations (*Dianthus*), and took forever to make, each carnation being taken to pieces and reassembled into groups of wired petals. The base would be a ball of moss, bound together with string, and sometimes covered with chicken wire, to support the many stems. The finished ball would often be very heavy because all the flowers would have to be wired into the moss.

Here I have used a Styrofoam ball. This way all you need to do is push the stems into the foam. Very little wiring is needed – the odd heavier flower should be glued in just to be sure it stays in place. The handle is ribbon secured with a long wire which is pushed right through the ball and turned up back into the foam like a hairpin, to stop the ribbon handle coming out.

At first it is easier to start the ball by holding it in your hand, leaving your other hand free to do the work, but after a little while you will need to ensure that it looks and stays round, and at this point I find it easier to hang it up to finish off. Start at the top working around, and finish by filling underneath. Here I have used mixed foliage: sage (*Salvia officinalis*), parsley (*Petroselinum crispum*), lavender cotton (*Santolina*), and spurge (*Euphorbia*). At the top are three yellow tulips interspersed with gypsophila (*G. paniculata*) and finally looped tulip leaves.

The horseshoe is another alternative for a younger flower girl to

THE FLOWERS

Lenten rose (*Helleborus orientalis*)

Gypsophila (*G. paniculata*)

Spurge or Laurel (*Euphorbia*)

Parsley (*Petroselinum crispum*)

Sage (*Salvia officinalis*)

Yellow tulips (*Tulipa*)

Lavender cotton (*Santolina*)

THE FLOWERS

Dried and silk polyester flowers

handle at the top. When you reach half way take another length of ribbon and start the procedure again, and when you come to the middle of this one tie the two ribbons together. Wire a bow and add center flowers to cover the join. To finish off you may need to mold it into shape gently with your hands to create the curved horseshoe. Tie the ribbons at the top into a handle, ensuring that they will not come undone.

A FLORAL HOOP AND CROWN

Young and pretty tartan, lifted by a crisp white shirt and cotton lace underskirt, is set off delightfully by brightly colored anemones. Hoops can be bought from florist shops in all sizes or you can make one yourself from a wire coat hanger and thick florist wire, binding it with plastic, round and round to create a thick hoop. To finish off cover the whole ring in green ribbon, gluing it every now and again to keep it in place. For the yellow, use a thin ribbon and bind around evenly again.

You can use fresh flowers, but these anemones are actually artificial, so the flower girl has a keepsake. Glue the anemones on in sections and wire on a cluster of trailing ribbons at the top.

To make the headpiece you need wire, foliage and flowers to match the hoop. The choice of flowers is yours and almost anything could be used here. Measure around the flower girl's head and make a wire frame from florist's wire to the correct size. Tape it, and using trailing foliage, twist pieces round and round until the circle is evenly covered. You may need to wire it every now and again to keep the foliage in place. Here I used a very long strand of golden ivy on top, twisting it around, and glued the anemones firmly into place. Using extra thin yellow ribbon, bound round the crown to match the hoop, finished it off perfectly. ॐ

THE FLOWERS

Ivy (*Hedera*)
Artificial anemones

THE *B*RIDE
& GROOM,
AND GUESTS

A CHRISTMAS CELEBRATION

A romantic bouquet of deep red roses, the symbol of love, surrounded by dark green giant fir (*Abies grandis*) foliage: so the bright red flowers bring a rich warmth to a crisp, cold season. Shiny golden edged holly (*Ilex aquifolium*) adds an extra Christmas sparkle.

A touch of tartan ribbon amongst the roses links it with the groom's vest, and the groom's boutonniere is a single red rose with giant fir foliage and a very small tartan bow just at the bottom, keeping the tartan flavor throughout. The young flower girl carries

THE FLOWERS

Deep red roses (*Rosa*)

Rose leaves

Holly (*Ilex aquifolium*)

Giant fir (*Abies grandis*) foliage

THE FLOWERS

Deep red roses (*Rosa*)

Rose leaves

Holly (*Ilex aquifolium*)

Giant fir (*Abies grandis*) foliage

a smaller version of the bride's handshower design, which matches perfectly. Both bouquets were assembled on foam holders (see pages 116–7). You can create a similar (and less expensive) effect by using other flowers among your roses, such as deep red freesias, spray carnations (*Dianthus*) or Peruvian lilies (*Alstroemeria*).

The bride's headpiece design is called a cabbage rose, made up from lots of roses. Remove the petals from a number of flowers, and wire them together in groups of two or three. Using a bud for the center, place the wired petals around its edge, working around and around the center and gradually making it bigger as you go, using binding wire to keep them all in place. Finish off by edging with individual rose leaves. Here the completed piece was sewn to the veil and pinned into the hair with hairpins.

$\mathcal{F}$LOWERS FOR THE GUESTS

A close family group enjoys the festivities at a Christmas wedding. Father's boutonniere is kept simple by using a single red rose surrounded by golden ivy (*Hedera*) leaves. Mother's handbag spray matches in color, with split carnations (*Dianthus*) and red roses finished off at one end with a pretty red and gold ribbon. A corsage of red roses, artificial berries and pieces of very thin tartan ribbon is worn by the other guest.

A handbag spray is made in the same way as a corsage, wiring all the leaves and flowers separately, taping and mounting them into groups. You need to make two corsages, joining them in the middle to make one piece with a returned end (see also the crescent bouquet on page 38). When you start you will need one long wire that measures twice the length of the handbag, plus a little extra to join under the handbag flap at the back. If your wire isn't long enough you will have to use two wires firmly twisted together. Tape your anchor wire first. Assemble the spray on your anchor wire, taping it into place as you go. When the spray is complete, and just before the ceremony, attach it to the bag and twist the wire tightly at the back, cutting off any sharp ends or bending them in, to ensure they do not scratch the bag. Do not attach the spray too soon as the handbag might be marked by water from the flowers.

CORSAGES AND BOUTONNIERES

A wedding is a time of celebration for everyone, when we all enjoy dressing for the occasion. Any outfit can be dressed up with flowers, and a corsage can be worn either on a suit or dress. If the dress fabric is too soft and flimsy, a handbag spray is a pretty alternative. A very plain hat can also be successfully decorated with flowers.

THE CORSAGE

Deep red roses (*Rosa*)

Artificial raspberries

Golden ivy (*Hedera*)

THE HANDBAG SPRAY

Deep red roses (*Rosa*)

Carnations (*Dianthus*)

Sprayed golden ivy (*Hedera*)

THE BOUTONNIERE

Deep red roses (*Rosa*)

Sprayed golden ivy (*Hedera*)

THE FLOWERS

Garden roses (*Rosa*)

Heather (*Erica*)

Ivy (*Hedera*)

(*Previous page*)

THE FLOWERS IN VASES

Grape hyacinths (*Muscari*)

Primrose (*Primula*)

Lungwort (*Pulmonaria*)

Spurge or Laurel (*Euphorbia*)

Rock cress (*Arabis*)

Pansy (*Viola*)

BOUTONNIERES AND CORSAGES

Gypsophila (*G. paniculata*)

Camellia

Primrose (*Primula*)

Heather (*Erica*)

Lenten rose (*Helleborus orientalis*)

For the men it has been the custom over the years to wear on their suit nothing but a single carnation in the buttonhole, but while this remains a classic, traditions are changing, and it is a pleasure to see a gentleman wearing a rose or gardenia and even gypsophila in his buttonhole. A few simple flowers picked from the garden can be just as effective, and if conditioned correctly will last well.

Boutonnieres and corsages should be laid out carefully before the wedding to save them from being damaged: here a pretty cake stand does the job. Simple gypsophila is tied with a white bow, and mingled with primroses (*Primula*) picked from the orchard the day before. Lenten roses (*Helleborus*) are tied with gold lace ribbon for a simple corsage. Pieces of heather (*Erica*) clustered together and tied at the base with white ribbon is something different for the groom to wear, and so is the single camellia bloom.

Nothing here is wired; all the flowers are left on their natural stems and tied with ribbon to secure them. A straight pin or small gold safety pin is all that is needed to attach the spray or boutonniere to the outfit.

For the tiny guest a small bag of sweets is decorated with a naturally tied bunch of grape hyacinths (*Muscari*), secured with a silver wire and then tied on with blue matching ribbon. You could use freesias or roses and gypsophila instead if you prefer, but the flowers need to be dainty and lightweight so that the child finds it easy to hold. If the ribbon should be too tight for the child to open the bag, you could sew the flower spray on instead of tying.

A couple of roses, small sprigs of heather (*Erica*) and ivy (*Hedera*) leaves picked from Grandmother's garden, together make a very pretty going-away corsage. The flowers tone wonderfully with the bride's tartan going-away outfit. These roses were pinned with silver wire to keep them closed and then mounted on thicker black wire. Silver wire makes a tiny stitch through the back of the ivy leaf and is gently twisted round the stem, which is finished off by taping. 🐦

ORCHIDS FOR THE BRIDE AND GROOM

Fresh and crisp orchids (*Phalaenopsis*) assembled together in a tiny simple bouquet. Not every bride will want to wear a traditional dress, but flowers can complement any outfit beautifully. You may decide to wear a simple corsage on your dress, or have a spray of flowers for your handbag, or even choose to carry a tiny, simple bouquet. This bride wears a short ivory suit with bead decoration on the bodice, and a beautiful hat. In her hand she carries a strikingly individual bouquet of fresh and crisp *Phalaenopsis* orchids, with a few pearl sprays dotted amongst prayer plant (*Maranta leuconera*), lonicera (*L. nitida*) and ivy (*Hedera*) foliage. This is a perfect assembly: nothing is exaggerated, just cool and understated. The groom wears an orchid from the bouquet in his buttonhole with camellia foliage behind.

This bouquet is wired and taped, with each flower wired through the head with thin silver wire. This takes a great deal of patience as orchids are extremely delicate and bruise very easily. Wire the leaves with a small stitch through the back using a silver wire, and then mount them on a black wire with tape, either in groups or singly. Using thin pieces of trailing ivy to start the bouquet work upwards from the trail, adding flowers as you go, securing each one with tape, or binding wire if preferred. I always opt for tape as this helps to keep the bouquet lightweight. Aim for an arrangement that is light, delicate, well-balanced and has movement.

When you reach the center, which will become the binding point, bend the wires down to form the handle. Position the flowers at the side and top, finally adding a perfect specimen for the focal point in the middle. To finish off add a few sprays of pearls in the center of the bouquet. You can of course use whichever flowers you choose: lilies would also be very striking. ❧

THE FLOWERS

Orchids (*Phalaenopsis*)

Lonicera (*L. nitida*) foliage

Ivy (*Hedera*)

Prayer plant (*Maranta leuconeura*)

Off to the Church

*L*ILIES IN A CARRIAGE

It is wonderfully romantic to travel to church on your wedding day in a horse and carriage! This very elegant two-seater promises a slow, stately journey, arriving at your destination in real style. It is even greater fun to decorate the carriage with flowers, forming the perfect complement to the bridal bouquet and color scheme. Two bunches of lily of the valley (*Convallaria majalis*), tied with a ribbon bow, adorn the gleaming brass coach lamps. The hood of the carriage is decorated with an oval design of daisies, lilies and ribbon.

Remember, whichever flowers you choose to decorate with, the weather may not always be good. The breeze is often a problem, so your floral decoration must be firmly fixed on, and it is best if the design is neat and compact.

The oval design on the hood of the carriage was assembled in a foam holder, in which it is necessary to glue your flowers, so they do not all drop out on the journey. The decoration itself is designed in the same way as the top half of a pew end (see page 83) and if you require trailing pieces, you can add them at the bottom. You can only use foam if there is something for you to attach it to firmly, and if there is not, then I suggest you use a tied bunch instead. This can then be secured with ribbon.

The bride's handshower of white Easter lilies (*Lilium longiflorum*) is laid softly on a veil on the seat of the carriage. This bouquet was designed in a floral foam holder with the outer flowers all glued into place. Foliage of butcher's broom (*Ruscus*) and ivy (*Hedera*) cascade, followed by young lily heads and buds. At the top of the bouquet the bell-like flowers of fringecups (*Tellima*) gush out from the left, and bunches of lily of the valley (*Convallaria majalis*) from the other side. Full heads of scented viburnum (*V. × carlcephalum*) add weight to the center.

These lilies have magnificent waxy blooms, shaped like trumpets

THE FLOWERS

Hebe (figwort shrub)

Ivy (*Hedera*)

Prairie gentians (*Eustoma grandiflorum*)

Heath (*Aster ericoïdes*)

Lily of the valley (*Convallaria majalis*)

bursting forth with joy. Their bright yellow pollen can easily mark your bloom, so just remove the stamens with your fingers before you start. Beware, because it is sticky and can be difficult to get off your fingers immediately: be very careful indeed that it does not mark the wedding dress.

THE FLOWERS

Fringecups (*Tellima*)

Scented viburnum (*V.* × *carlcephalum*)

Ivy (*Hedera*)

Butcher's broom (*Ruscus*)

Lily of the valley (*Convallaria majalis*)

Easter lilies (*Lilium longiflorum*)

VINTAGE GOLDEN BEAUTY

THE FLOWERS

White tulips (*Tulipa*)

Double yellow tulips (*Tulipa*)

Snowball bush (*Viburnum opulus* "Roseum")

Broom (*Genista*)

Lilac (*Syringa vulgaris*)

The bride's spring handshower laid on the running board of the Rolls Royce reflects its golden beauty in the shiny paintwork.

Even the spare wheel of a 1931 vintage Rolls Royce can be bedecked with flowers! Broom (*Genista*), tulips and white lilac (*Syringa vulgaris*) are arranged in a fan shape on a sticky-backed floral foam pad, which is pushed against the spokes. If the spokes were not upright you might need to add an anchor wire at the

THE FLOWERS

Euonymus (*E. fortunei*)

Broom (*Genista*)

Lilac (*Syringa vulgaris*)

Double yellow tulips (*Tulipa*)

White tulips (*Tulipa*)

bottom as well as a supporting wire to attach the top flower to the wheel, using taped wires so as not to scratch the paint work. Glue the flowers into the damp foam base so that they all stay in place on the journey. If you use just a very small amount of foliage, the arrangement appears to be bursting with flowers. ✒

FLOWERS FOR A SIMPLE CHURCH

In this simple, modern church, two arrangements in brass church vases decorate each side of the altar. Floral foam must be carved to fit the vases before the arranging could commence. The arrangements are light and airy with very little foliage, small sprigs of ivy (*Hedera*) tumble forward concealing part of the vases. A matching display stands at the base of the alter flowing on to the deep blue carpet.

Two tied bunches of gypsophila (*G. paniculata*) and foliage are secured with ribbon to the ends of the choir stalls. To construct this kind of pew end, first decide how long you want the pew ends to be, remembering that each spray will have to look the same. For this natural tied design, lay your foliage, and then some gypsophila, on a table and tie with string. Gather the bunch up in your hand and gradually add a few more sprigs of plant material and gypsophila, building up a more solid tied bunch. Finish by tying with matching ribbon, leaving tails long enough to tie behind the pew end. ❧

ALTAR FLOWERS

Gypsophila (*G. paniculata*)

Spray carnations (*Dianthus*)

Larkspur (*Delphinium*)

Gum tree (*Eucalyptus*)

Ivy (*Hedera*)

Butcher's broom (*Ruscus*)

THE FLOWERS

Spray carnations (*Dianthus*)

Hebe (figwort shrub)

Bear grass (*Dasylirion*)

Ivy (*Hedera*)

Silver *Centaurea*

Gypsophila (*G. paniculata*)

Lilac-colored freesias

Larkspur (*Delphinium*)

An Arrangement for the Font

A selection of fresh, natural summer flowers is laid on top of this beautifully carved font. The flowers could easily have been picked from the garden; the lush green ivy (*Hedera*), bear grass (*Dasylirion*) and larkspur (*Delphinium*) buds spurt forth out of the center and side of this wild design. I used a flat floral foam pad as my base; they are available from most good florist shops and garden centers, but if you cannot find one, a dish and floral foam will do the job just as well. The flowers are white larkspur, spray carnations (*Dianthus*) and heavily perfumed lilac-colored freesias. Lashings of gypsophila (*G. paniculata*) give the light and airy appearance. As churches are often very dark you may find that paler colors look more effective.

THE FLOWERS

Carnations (*Dianthus*)

Chrysanthemums (*Dendranthema*)

Brompton stock (*Matthiola incana*)

Larkspur (*Delphinium*)

Peruvian lilies (*Alstroemeria*)

Transvaal daisies (*Gerbera*)

Gypsophila (*G. paniculata*)

Gum tree (*Eucalyptus*)

Bear grass (*Dasylirion*)

Ferns (*Arachniodes*)

Ivy (*Hedera*)

A PEDESTAL ARRANGEMENT

A pedestal arrangement can seem a daunting task for many people, because of the sheer size. It has to be constructed so that it balances well and does not appear top-heavy. The secret is to ensure that you have a good foundation and that there is enough floral foam. Tape a piece of wire netting securely across the top and wire it underneath to add stability. Use foliage to make your outline, and once you have a good shape your flowers will stay within the framework.

You will need to give your arrangement a "skirt," spiralling downward out of the design, so that the flowers do not look as if they have simply been plopped on top of the pedestal container. The aim is to make your flowers and container into one complete design, forming a line together.

For this arrangement start with a foliage outline, and create a cascade of foliage from underneath, using a number of stems of ivy (*Hedera*) and fine strips of bear grass (*Dasylirion*). Then build in the flowers, maintaining the balance. Peruvian lily (*Alstroemeria*) has lots of heads on one stem making it good value for the money. This very attractive flower is most useful in arrangements like this and comes in many color shades. Larkspur (*Delphinium*) has a straighter, more elegant blossom, as does the Brompton stock (*Matthiola incana*), which is also strongly scented. Stems of chrysanthemums (*Dendranthema*) add weight to the display and Transvaal daisies (*Gerbera*) give more solid blooms. These need to be gently wired on green mounting wire to give support, as they tend to twist and bend naturally otherwise. Add sprigs of gypsophila (*G. paniculata*) last, to give the finished arrangement a soft, misty look.

FLOWERS FOR A COUNTRY CHURCH

This small country church is decorated quite simply with cream and white flowers.

A facing arrangement (see pages 121–2) stands on the chancel steps, its height calculated just to reach the top of the choir stalls, so as not to overwhelm the church with flowers. The foliage of dark green butcher's broom (*Ruscus*), golden privet (*Ligustrum ovalifolium*), bay tree (*Laurus nobilis*), laurustinus (*Viburnum tinus*), wild ivy (*Hedera*), spurge (*Euphorbia*) and hebe would alone make a striking array, there is such a strong variation of greens. But sprays of white heath (*Aster ericoïdes*), double chrysanthemum (*Dendranthema*) sprays and prairie gentians (*Eustoma grandiflorum*) all different in texture and shape add a lot of interesting light to the display, which in these dark surroundings is crucial.

I started off this design by positioning the top sprays of foliage first and then grading downwards. The ivy and butcher's broom at the bottom of the design creates a flowing movement down over the stone steps. A similar design arranged in a black flat dish stands on the beautifully twisted wooden pedestal. Here I have tried to introduce even more movement and fall by tumbling the foliage forward, using all of its natural formation. A pedestal design will always give you more scope, as there is so much space that can be used around your design.

The flowers on the pew ends are displayed in a special container, which has been designed with this job in mind and is available from florists. It has a curved plastic arm which neatly fits over the wood of the pew. Made in a dark green, it looks like wrought iron, but is actually plastic with a soft pad at the back to protect the wood. At the front there is a plastic cage containing floral foam, which needs only to be lightly moistened so that water does not drip on the floor. If you are unable to make the pew ends *in situ* then hook them over a

THE FLOWERS

Heath (*Aster ericoïdes*)

Double chrysanthemum (*Dendranthema*) sprays

Prairie gentians (*Eustoma grandiflorum*)

Hebe (figwort shrub)

Butcher's broom (*Ruscus*)

Ivy (*Hedera*)

Golden privet (*Ligustrum ovalifolium*)

Laurustinus (*Viburnum tinus*)

90

THE FLOWERS

Easter lilies (*Lilium longiflorum*)

Heath (*Aster ericoïdes*)

Hebe (figwort shrub)

Ivy (*Hedera*)

Prairie gentians (*Eustoma grandiflorum*)

Viburnum (*V. × carlcephalam*)

cupboard door in the kitchen. You will need to use one as a model to copy from: it is important to keep all the lengths and widths the same, otherwise, *en masse*, they will look uneven in church.

Pew end containers are very easy to use. Start with the foliage to disguise the cage and foam, and then position the bottom flowers, having first decided how long they are to be. Pay particular attention to the sides, as they will be seen as everyone walks up the aisle. Here I have worked them into a teardrop shape. Make your outline first, then work toward the middle, adding the lily heads last of all, as they are the focal flowers. Lightly spray each one, making sure that you do not damage any surrounding wood. I find it easier to put a sheet of plastic behind each one before I spray.

The altar flowers are just placed in brass vases filled with water. The graceful Easter lilies (*Lileum longiflorum*) twist and curve naturally, so there is no need to use complicated methods to display them. ⬥

FLOWERS FOR CELEBRATIONS

WEDDING GIFTS AND FAVORS

PARCEL SPRAYS

Freesias

Heather (*Erica*)

Daffodils (*Narcissus*)

Gypsophila (*G. paniculata*)

Carnations (*Dianthus*)

Goldenrod (*Solidago*)

THE LARGE ARRANGEMENT

Sword fern (*Nephrolepis exaltata*)

Pittosporum foliage

Ivy (*Hedera*)

Jerusalem sage (*Phlomis fruticosa*)

White heather (*Erica*)

White chrysanthemums
(*Dendranthema*)

Spray chrysanthemums
(*Dendranthema*)

Cream orchids (*Dendrobium*)

A beautiful and special touch, decorating your wedding gift with flowers is also strikingly unusual. A bottle of champagne is always a very welcome gift but is never an easy thing to wrap well, so instead of using a box or bottle bag, why not be distinctive, and decorate the bottle itself with flowers? All you need is a sticky-backed floral foam pad, which should be available from a good florist's shop or garden center. Just place your foliage and flowers into the dampened foam as you would if you were designing any small arrangement. In mine I placed the flowers in such a way to make them look like a tied bunch: to achieve that effect place the flowers in a fan shape facing one way and then push the spare stems into the other end, concealing your trick with a little foliage. At the point where the flowers and stalks meet add a ribbon bow to complete your gift spray. To secure the flowers to the bottle just remove the tape from the back and press the sticky pad firmly down on a dry surface; if your bottle has been in the fridge it may not stick to the glass, so you will have to place it on the bottle label instead.

Use another dampened sticky-backed foam pad for the other parcel spray. (Do not saturate the foam or it will part company from the sticky base.) When designing your nosegay, remember to use the foam pad in the same way as you would use floral foam for any arrangement, and you won't go wrong. Apart from the usual ribbon bow you can also pretty up a parcel with dried and silk flowers, wiring them together in the same way as a corsage. You could even design it in such a way that it would make an attractive wall decoration afterward. Another very simple idea is to pick a small bunch of heather (*Erica*) from the garden and tie it with ribbon to make a spray. Heather lasts quite well out of water and will not wilt.

The impressive white and cream arrangement on the wedding gift table is surprisingly inexpensive to make. It contains only six white

single chrysanthemum (*Dendranthema*) sprays and two generous spray chrysanthemums: broken down into individual blooms they go a long way. The white heather came from the garden, as did the foliage. For just a little touch of luxury there is one bunch of cream orchids (*Dendrobium*). Of course this container is very beautiful and in itself quite expensive, but you can of course use something simpler.

Tape floral foam into the top of your container, down the sides and across the top of the dish to keep it securely in place. As usual make the outline first with foliage creating a general shape, then position the highest flowers, then the side ones, and gradually build up the middle, adding the heather and orchids last, cascading out from the sides and front. Remember to leave a space at the back for watering the foam before you finish off with foliage. The back of an arrangement like this must always look as neat as the front, especially in this case where it can be viewed in the mirror behind.

FAVORS

Pretty individual favors, filled with sugared almonds and placed in a basket, are handed to all the female guests by the bride as a symbol of good luck. You can buy these in kit form; all you have to provide is the sugared almonds.

A bride's fan is another alternative to a floral bouquet. To assemble this design, use miniature spray roses, surrounded by Peruvian lilies (*Alstroemeria*) with small pieces of beargrass and ivy (*Hedera*) foliage in tiny trailing pieces trickling out from beneath the flowers. You can create this small spray in the same way as a corsage, wiring it with silver wires and taping. To secure it in place sew the completed spray to the fan. A matching headpiece can also be wired together and sewn to the top of the comb on the veil. ❧

(*Previous page*)

THE FLOWERS

Peruvian lilies (*Alstroemeria*)

Miniature spray roses (*Rosa*)

Ivy (*Hedera*)

Bear grass (*Dasylirian*)

ORCHIDS ON A CAKE

THE FLOWERS

Orchids (*Phalaenopsis*)
Ivy (*Hedera*)

The cake usually stands on a separate table where it can be seen as a feature, so it is a nice idea to decorate the cake table with a pretty matching cloth, ribbons and flowers. There are some extremely talented cake decorators who can create the most wonderful floral displays from icing, and you may decide not to have fresh flowers on your cake at all. However if you do choose to have fresh flowers there are many ways they can be arranged. You could use a pretty sherry or wine glass, and arrange a few flowers in it very simply. You can make or order a tiny replica of your bouquet to be placed into a silver cake vase. Pieces of trailing ivy with a flower dotted here and there also looks very attractive.

Flowers can even come to the rescue if some disaster befalls the cake! I remember one occasion when the bakery had ruined a bride's cake by icing it in the wrong color. I made up twelve small tied bunches of dainty flowers, each one tied with very thin ribbon. Out of the top of each bunch trailed thin strands of ivy. On the morning of the wedding I laid a bunch on each corner of the three-tiered cake, leaving the ivy to trickle down over the edge. The stalks of each bunch met in the middle of the cake, almost covering the icing with flowers. In the end the finished decorations were extremely pretty, and no one was any the wiser!

Here, on a rather ornate cake, I have used simple but striking orchids (*Phalaenopsis*). For the top tier they have been inserted into a floral foam pad, like the ones I used on the parcel sprays, although this time I have not peeled off the sticky back. For the middle and bottom tier, flowers and trailing ivy (*Hedera*) have simply been laid on the cake. These will last quite well out of water, but it is worth leaving this job until one of the last, to ensure maximum freshness. I wired and taped the remaining orchids and ivy into small sprays and pinned them directly to the cloth, to finish off the table decoration. 🐋

A FLORAL LUNCHEON AT HOME

This floral display for a small, intimate wedding breakfast at home is designed on a candelabra. Using a candle cup which fits into the top of the middle arm of the candlestick, begin by taping in a round piece of floral foam. Tape the foam into the cup slightly off center, then across the other way leaving space for the candle to go in the middle. Push your candle in next and then start to outline your arrangement with foliage.

A cascading design is perfect, as this arrangement will be seen from underneath as well as all around. It is important that you select flowers which blend well together: fragrant blossom is a delightful bonus and will be appreciated by all who are seated at your wedding breakfast. Build up the flowers gradually, using the larger flowers in recess and the daintier ones on longer stems flowing outward. Finally put the other two candles into position and make any final adjustments.

Do not make the arrangement too large or overpowering: the guests must be able to converse over the flowers. Here there is a fine string of silver beads leading out from the arrangement to each guest's place-setting, finishing at their place card with an orchid tied with a silver bow.

If you have arranged your flowers the day before the wedding, store them in a cool place and make sure they are filled with water. Take care not to spray water on the silver as this will mark and cause you unnecessary cleaning work. ❧

THE FLOWERS

Fresh porcelain roses (*Rosa*)

Orchids (*Dendrobium*)

Peruvian lilies (*Alstroemeria*)

Freesias

Broom (*Genista*)

Spray carnations (*Dianthus*)

Orchids (*Cymbidium*)

Gum tree (*Eucalyptus*)

Hebe (figwort shrub)

102

$\mathcal{S}$TRAWBERRY TEA

This summer celebration in the garden is set off beautifully by this arrangement, displayed in a cut glass, stemmed candy dish, which elevated the design up off the table. Use one-third of a brick of floral foam, taped across the dish twice to stop it moving about. You can use a floral foam frog with sticky clay on the bottom for extra support. Place it on the bottom of your dish and push down to ensure that it is stuck firmly, then place the foam down on the plastic prongs.

This design is a large all round nosegay, since it can be seen from all sides. First use trails of ivy (*Hedera*) to spill out over the edge, touching the cloth. Then make the outline of the design with spray carnation buds (*Dianthus*), working around the outer edge, then up towards the center. Add the full heads of lilies. Cut them from a large stem, containing a number of blooms. Then add the peach and red garden roses. Their heads are quite large, so in order that they are not too dominant, place them in recess. Dot tiny sprigs of scented honeysuckle (*Lonicera periclymenum*) here and there. Then, finally, to fill in, position clusters of lady's mantle (*Alchemilla*) and gypsophila (*G. paniculata*), to give a light, airy look to the arrangement.

The tablecloth decoration is made up of lady's mantle, gypsophila, spray carnations and single rose heads. To assemble these all you have to do is tie the lady's mantle and gypsophila together forming a bunch with a ribbon bow. Be quite generous with your material so that you obtain a full, fluffy effect. You will need two of these to go across the center front of the cloth. Tie the two stalk ends together and place a ribbon bow at the center, so you end up with a double-ended tied bunch. For the end pieces, construct two more bunches in the same way, but this time add a stem of spray carnation. Pin the two corner bunches to the corners of the tablecloth, so that they hang down. Then pin the middle, double-ended bunch horizontally in the

THE FLOWERS

Lilies (*Lilium*)

Spray carnations (*Dianthus*)

Peach roses (*Rosa*)

Red roses (*Rosa*)

Ivy (*Hedera*)

Beech (*Fagus*) leaves

Gypsophila (*G. paniculata*)

Lady's mantle (*Alchemilla*)

Honeysuckle (*Lonicera periclymenum*)

middle. This will need a couple of pins on each side to keep it in place. The roses should be added last, so that you can make sure it all looks balanced. Wire the roses singly, leaving a long stem on each one, and then tape, covering the wires. Push the wire down into the corner bunches and then bend the wire back up again to secure the rose. Follow the same instructions for the center rose, but this time wind the wire around the horizontal tied bunch, making sure that no wire is visible. Ideally, this needs to be done at the last minute. Spray a little water on each bunch to keep them fresh, but be sure not to wet the cloth. ᨠ

STEP-BY-STEP TECHNIQUES

A BOUTONNIERE

You will need a carnation, thin silver wire and black or green florists' wire, tape and a pin.

Using a single carnation, first cut the stem quite short as shown. Push a wire up inside the stem until it comes through the center of the flower. Bend the top of the wire into a small hook and then gently pull it back down into the center of the flower.

Take three leaves from the carnation, or use ivy or fern if you prefer. Wire the leaves together at the bottom with a silver wire, and cover the wire with tape. Place the group of leaves behind the carnation and tape them together right to the bottom of the wire; then cut the wire to the required length.

Bend the wired stem just underneath the flower head, so that when it is put into the buttonhole it will look part of the outfit and not just stuck in. If there is no buttonhole in the suit, the flower can be pinned behind the lapel to hide the stem. ৵

A ROSE CORSAGE

You will need two or three roses, ivy leaves and other foliage of your choice, tape, thin silver wire, florists' wire, a pin to keep the corsage in place on the outfit, and a ribbon bow to finish off.

Wire each rose by inserting a wire up into the stem, and then tape each one separately. If it is a very hot day you may need to pin each rose to stop it opening. Do this by making very small hair pins out of silver wire. Take one and pin through the green sepal into the rose head, gently holding it as firmly closed as possible. Continue around the rose until you have a firmly closed bud.

Wire your ivy leaves by making a tiny stitch in the back of the leaf with thin silver wire: carefully pierce the leaf either side of the vein, then bring both ends of wire down to meet each other and twist around the natural stem at the base of the leaf.

Tape all your material first. It is important to use tape (rather than binding wire) to keep your design as light and dainty as possible: no one wants to wear an ugly heavy corsage that would pull a suit or dress out of shape.

Start assembling the corsage at the top with a small leaf, fern and the smaller rose bud. Gradually work down, finishing with the larger roses and leaves at the bottom. Introduce your foliage a piece at a time to cradle the rose heads.

To complete the corsage finish off with a simple ribbon bow. Finally cut off excess wires. ✐

A *B*RIDE'S OR FLOWER GIRL'S HEADPIECE

You will need a hot glue gun, a selection of flowers and foliage and a hair band. Flowers tend to stick better to a covered headband, obtainable from a florist or a florist supply warehouse, than to a plain plastic band; alternatively buy a plastic one and cover it with ribbon. Always keep a bowl of water on one side for your own safety when using the glue gun, in case you burn yourself.

Before you cut off the flower heads, lay the headband down and work out how many blossoms you will need to cover the band so that you do not cut off too many and waste them.

Cover the band first with ivy leaves or other foliage leaves, overlapping them as you go round. Glue each one and

press it gently on the band, allow to dry for a few seconds and then press again firmly into place.

When you reach the middle turn the band around and start at the other end, so that you maintain a symmetry, with both sides meeting in the center.

Now add the flowers, starting with a bud at one end of the band and gluing each piece as before.

When you reach the middle, again start at the other end and work back into the center, finishing with a full bloom for the focal point.

To make a complete crown use two headbands and glue them together to make a circle of the correct size. Follow the instructions for the headband, but start at the back this time, working round to the center front. When you have reached this point return to the back and work round the other side, finishing off with a central bloom. ❧

A *H*ANDSHOWER BOUQUET

You will need a glue gun, a foam bouquet holder, ivy and other foliage, flowers, and a bottle half filled with sand to weigh it down. You may need to wire the ivy trails, and softer stemmed flowers should be wired for extra support.

Using the bottle makes this just like creating an arrangement, and it gives you the opportunity to look directly at your piece of work through all the making up stages. It also saves damaging the flowers as there is no need to remove the bouquet from the bottle until the design is completed.

Place the bouquet holder in the bottle and start by glueing foliage around the edge of the holder, choosing longer pieces for the bottom trail. The shape you are aiming for resembles a tear drop. Cover the top of the foam with lighter, softer foliage to conceal the base, gluing the thicker pieces. Each piece must be pushed firmly into the foam.

Now add the flowers. Follow your foliage outline completing the outer edge of your bouquet first using buds and smaller flowers. It may be useful to support wire the longer flowers, and it is important to glue all these into place. Build up to the finished piece using a flower at a time and gluing where necessary.

Finish off by adding some perfect flower heads in the center of the design to create a focal point. Keep the focal flowers or center ones fairly short.

There is no need to worry about the handle as good bouquet holders already have a neat ribbon handle. Look at the back to make sure that you cannot see any glue or foam showing: if you can, just cover by adding small stems of foliage. You can put a small ribbon bow in at the back to neaten it off, but this is not really necessary. Spray the back and front with fresh water, place the bouquet in a box, cover with plastic and store in a cool room. If you leave anything uncovered, the water will evaporate and the flowers will wilt. If anything should wilt, spray with water and cover completely with plastic, and leave for a few hours; or replace the wilted piece. ৯৩

A FLOWER GIRL'S NOSEGAY

You will need a selection of flowers, thin silver wire and black or green florists' wire, silver binding wire, tape to cover the wires and a pair of scissors.

This is a wired hand posy. Each flower and piece of foliage needs to be wired and then taped.

Divide the flowers into five groups and wire them into units, assembling them as you would a corsage, using tape, but this time leave the long wires on.

Gather the five sections up into your hand, hold the long wires and bend each unit of flowers over your hand, forming a circle. At the point where you have bent the flower units over your hand it may be necessary to use some florist's binding wire at the top of the handle, wrapping it around the other wires a few times just to keep them all in place. Cut off any excess binding wire and return to tape to keep your design light.

Now place individual flowers into the top of the nosegay, filling in any gaps, and keep two or three special blooms for the center. Tape the long wires together to form a handle and cut off any wires that are not required. Remember to leave enough of a handle for the flower girl to hold. A good guide is to hold the design in your hand, wrapping your fingers around the wire handle.

Leave an inch below your little
finger, and cut off any wires
that are left: this should then be
a comfortable length to hold.
Finish off by covering the
handle with ribbon. ≥∾

A FRONT-FACING ARRANGEMENT

You will need a dish, a pair of scissors, a piece of floral foam, tape and a selection of flowers and foliage of your choice.

Cut your foam to the correct size for the container, soak it, and then tape it into your dish or container. Tape across from side to side and back to front forming a cross.

Mark out the shape of your arrangement with dainty stems of foliage, and start to cover up the foam.

Now start to add the flowers, using buds and smaller flowers on the outside. Position the larger flowers towards the center making sure you also balance the colors. Use some flowers in recess (cut short, and pushed deep into the arrangement) to give your design interest and remember to choose colors that blend well together and with the color scheme for the wedding.

Finish off by covering the back of the display with foliage, leaving enough room to water the foam. When finished, spray the arrangement with a water mister to keep the flowers fresh. ❧

${\mathscr{A}}$CKNOWLEDGMENTS

It would have been impossible to put this book together without the help of very many people, and to all of them, I send my heartfelt thanks. In particular, I am most grateful to:

Alison Hemming and Helen Biddulph at Singular Sensation (8 Boldmere Road, Sutton Coldfield), for all their generous help in making bridesmaids dresses, and for the loan of most of the wedding gowns;

Brian and Marilyn Hill at Brian Hill Menswear (45 Boldmere Road, Sutton Coldfield), for providing the gentlemen's outfits, and for all their support;

Stewart Downie (87 Jockey Road, Sutton Coldfield), for the photographs;

Tony Ward (A.P. Ward, 31 Monmouth Drive, Sutton Coldfield), for all his help with the flowers;

Stanley and Daphne Dodds, Charlotte Downie, Debbie Edwards, Karen Edinburgh, Melanie Gudgin, Mitchell Hill, Leila Ivers, Chris and Archie Ross, Ann Stiles and Sheila Watson for modelling in the photographs;

Also the children who modelled: Gabrielle Barnes, Alex and Rory Edwards, Amy Summerton, and Lisa and Oliver Tonks;

The vicars of Streetly Methodist Church and St Mary the Virgin, Weeford, for permission to decorate the churches and take photographs;

Anne Adams, John Bradley, Daphne Dodds, Debbie Edwards, Nicola Evans, Bram Pitcher, Mary and Maurice Simmons and Sheila Watson for the loan of accessories;

Veronica Sorenson for her help and the loan of the wedding veil with Bucks Point lace edging;

Peter Henderson (9 Redacre Road, Boldmere, Sutton Coldfield), for providing and chauffeuring the Rolls Royce;

Derek and Dorinda Dixon (Chase Farm, Weeford Road, Roughley, Sutton Coldfield), for their kindness, and their care and patience with the horse and carriage;

Ian and Jackie Chapman at Fleetwoods Delicatessen (51–3 Boldmere Road, Sutton Coldfield), for the lovely wedding cake;

Chris Ryder International (230–2 Burton Road, Woodville, Burton-on-Trent), for supplying the bon-bonnière;

David at Oddfellows (16 Main Street, Shenstone), for little Bo-Peep's hairstyling;

David and Anne Adams, John and Rosemary Barnes, Chris and Rod Blake, Brian and Anne Sendall, and Angela and Reg Swaby for the loan of venues, and Lol Wakefield for the lambs.

Finally, but most importantly, a very special thanks to Chris, Lisa and Oliver for all their love, help and support; and to all my family and friends for their encouragement.

$\mathscr{I}$NDEX

artificial flowers   46
availability of flowers   13

baskets   42–5, 48–9
bouquets
   choice of flowers   13
   a Christmas celebration   64–6
   Christmas foliage   22–3
   Edwardian elegance   20–1
   in a field of flax   48–9
   floral foam holders   11, 12
   fun on the farm   46
   a golden haze   28–30
   hand-tied bouquet   26–7
   handshower bouquet   116–17
   harvest flame   31–3
   lilies   26–7, 74–9
   orchids   71
   see also nosegays
boutonnieres
   carnation   111
   choice of flowers   70
   Christmas   64, 67
   making   111
   orchid   71
bows   11
bridal fairs   12
bridal flowers
   bride's bedroom   24–5
   bride's fan   100
   freesias and rosebuds   38–9
   prayer book spray   36–7
   see also bouquets; headpieces;
     nosegays

cake, decorating with flowers   101
candles   15

car, flowers for the   80–2
carnations   7, 111, 120
carriage, flowers for the   74–9
checklist of materials   10–11
church flowers
   altar flowers   14, 93
   church flower committee   14
   color choice   15
   country church   90–3
   font arrangement   86
   front-facing arrangements   90,
     121–2
   pedestal arrangements   14, 88, 90
   pew ends   14, 83, 90–3
   simple modern church   83
clematis   13
color choice   12, 15
containers   10
corsages
   Christmas   67
   going-away corsage   70
   making   112–13
   rose corsage   112–13
countdown to the wedding
   day   16–17
courthouse wedding   14

daisies   7
dried flowers   20

fan   100
favors   100
floral foam   10, 11, 12
floral foam frogs   10
florists   11,12
florists' wire   10

flower girls
   baskets   42–5, 48–9
   a Christmas celebration   64–6
   in a field of flax   48–9
   floral hoop and crown   59–61
   flowers and pearls   55
   freesias and rosebuds   38–9
   a golden haze   30
   Little Bo-Peep   50–1
   nosegays   118–20
   pomander balls and
     horseshoes   56–8
flower preservative   13
foliage
   bridal bouquet   22–3
   conditioning   13, 15
   for the reception   15
   supplies of   10
freesias   13, 38–9

gardenias   7
gilded flowers   20
gluing the flowers   12, 114–15
groom, flowers for *see* boutonnieres
guests, flowers for   67–70

hand-tied bouquets   26–7
handbag spray   67
handshower bouquet   116–17
headpieces
   cabbage rose   66
   Christmas foliage   22–3
   crowns   7, 30, 31, 34–5, 46, 59–61,
     115
   flowers and pearls   55
   a golden haze   30

harvest flame   31
making   114–15
perfumed crown   34–5
sprays   20, 42, 55
honeysuckle   13
hoops   7, 59–61
horseshoes   56–8

language of flowers   7
lilies   7, 26–7, 74–9
lily of the valley   7, 13, 36–7

nosegays
   flowers and pearls   52–5
   making   118–20

orchids   71, 101
ordering and collecting the
   flowers   12

pampas grass   15
picking garden flowers   13
planning the flowers
   bouquets   13
   for the ceremony   14–15

checklist of materials   10–11
choosing the flowers   12–13
conditioning the flowers and
   foliage   13–14
consulting a florist   11, 12
countdown to the wedding
   day   16–17
for the reception   15
recruiting helpers   10
sharing the cost   14
pomander balls   56–8
prayer book spray   36–7

reception
   floral luncheon   102–3
   foliage, use of   15
   strawberry tea   104–7
   table centers   15
   wedding gift table   96–100
ribbon   11, 28, 30
ringbearers
   in a field of flax   48
   fun on the farm   46
rosebuds   38–9
roses   7, 13, 112–13

shepherd's crook   50–1
silver wire   11
stephanotis   13
symbolism   7

table decorations
   floral luncheon   102–3
   strawberry tea   104–7
   table centers   15
   tablecloth decoration   104–7

water mister   13–14
wedding gifts
   decorating with flowers   96
   wedding gift table   96–100
wholesale markets   11
wilting flowers   12
wires   10–11
wiring flowers   28, 36, 71, 112,
   118–19